JORDA

POCKET GUIDE

2023

Your Comprehensive Guide to Discovering the Wonders of The Jewel of the Middle East: Everything You Need to Know to Plan the Perfect Trip to Jordan.

Aliyah Malik

Copyright

Table of Contents

Copyright
Table of Contents
Introduction
Chapter 1: Discovering Jordan
        Geography And Climate
        Brief History
        Ancient Legends and Biblical Sites
Chapter 2: Jordan Travel Essentials
Chapter 3: Planning Your Itinerary
        3-Day Itinerary:
        7-Day Itinerary:
        10-Day Itinerary:
        14-Day Itinerary:
        21-Day Itinerary:
Chapter 4: Where to Stay
Chapter 5: Amman and Jerash
Chapter 6: Petra and Wadi Rum
Chapter 7: Aqaba
Chapter 8: The Dead Sea, Madaba and Mount Nebo
Chapter 9: Dana Biosphere Reserve and Shobak Castle
Chapter 10: Umm Qais, Ajloun Castle and Ma'in Hot Springs

Chapter 11: Dining and Local Cuisine
    Traditional Jordanian Dishes:
    Popular Restaurants and Street Food Markets:
Chapter 12: Shopping and Souvenirs
Chapter 13 Local Events and Festivals:
Conclusion
Glossary

Introduction

Step into the land where dreams merge with reality, where ancient tales are etched into towering cliffs, and where the warmth of hospitality embraces you like a long-lost friend. Welcome to Jordan, a treasure trove of wonder and enchantment waiting to be unveiled.

As you traverse this captivating kingdom, prepare to be transported through time. Imagine standing in awe before the rose-red city of Petra, its majestic facades carved into the very heart of the mountains. Feel the echoes of history reverberate through the winding Siq, whispering tales of lost civilizations and forgotten splendor. In Jordan, the past breathes, and its secrets are yours to discover.

But Jordan is more than just a land of mesmerizing ruins. It is a realm of contrasting landscapes, where the fiery sands of Wadi Rum stretch as far as the eye can see, where the turquoise waters of the Red Sea invite you to dive into a world of vibrant marine life, and where the stillness of the Dead Sea cradles you in its salty embrace, defying gravity and washing away worldly cares.

Beyond its natural wonders, Jordan is a tapestry of cultural richness. Engage with the Bedouin tribes, proud guardians of age-old traditions, and let their stories weave into the fabric of your own journey. Savor the tantalizing flavors of Jordanian cuisine, from the aromatic spices of a sizzling mansaf to the delicate sweetness of a freshly brewed cup of sage tea. Allow the sounds of music and dance to transport you to a world of vibrant celebration, where the rhythmic beats of the dabkeh unite hearts and spirits.

But perhaps the true magic of Jordan lies in its people. The Jordanians, with their genuine warmth and boundless hospitality, will embrace you as family. They will welcome you with open arms, eager to share their customs, their traditions, and their stories. In their company, you will feel a sense of belonging, a connection that transcends boundaries and reminds us of our shared humanity.

So, dear traveler, embark on a journey of a lifetime. Let Jordan's landscapes ignite your spirit, its history ignite your imagination, and its people ignite your soul. Allow yourself to be captivated, moved, and forever transformed by the land that whispers of forgotten kingdoms, timeless beauty, and the enduring power of human connection. Welcome to Jordan, where dreams come alive and memories are etched in the very fabric of your being.

Chapter 1: Discovering Jordan

Jordan, officially known as the Hashemite Kingdom of Jordan, is a sovereign country located in the heart of the Middle East. It spans an area of approximately 89,342 square kilometers and is home to a population of around 10 million people.

Jordan is a constitutional monarchy with King Abdullah II as the current reigning monarch. The government operates under a parliamentary system, where the King is the head of state, and the Prime Minister is the head of government. The legislative branch consists of a bicameral parliament, comprising the House of Representatives and the Senate.

The Jordanian people, known as Jordanians, are a diverse blend of ethnic and tribal backgrounds, reflecting the country's rich history and location at the crossroads of ancient civilizations. The majority of the population is Arab, with various Bedouin tribes, Circassians, and Chechens also contributing to the cultural fabric.

Hospitality is deeply ingrained in Jordanian culture, and visitors are warmly welcomed by the locals. Jordanians take pride in their traditions and customs, and their warmth and generosity are often expressed through sharing meals, offering tea, and engaging in heartfelt conversations.

The official language is Arabic, and Islam is the predominant religion, with the majority of Jordanians identifying as Sunni Muslims. However, Jordan is known for its religious tolerance, and other faiths, such as Christianity and Judaism, are also practiced by minority communities.

Jordanians have a strong sense of national pride and are known for their resilience and adaptability. The country's history, geographical diversity, and cultural heritage are celebrated through traditional music, dance, art, and culinary traditions.

Overall, the Jordanian people embrace a harmonious coexistence of modernity and tradition, and their warm and welcoming nature leaves a lasting impression on visitors, creating a sense of connection and appreciation for the country and its people.

Geography And Climate

Jordan, located in the heart of the Middle East, boasts a diverse geography and a climate that varies from region to region.

Geographically, Jordan is characterized by a mix of rugged mountains, fertile valleys, and arid desert landscapes. The western portion of the country is dominated by the Jordan Rift Valley, which extends from the Dead Sea in the south to the Sea of Galilee in the north. The eastern region is characterized by the vast Arabian Desert, with its vast stretches of sand dunes and rocky outcrops.

The country's most notable geographic feature is the Dead Sea, a saltwater lake situated in the Jordan Rift Valley. It is the lowest point on Earth and known for its high salt content, which allows people to effortlessly float on its surface.

In the north, the landscape is mountainous, with the Ajloun Highlands and the rolling hills of the Jordanian Plateau. The highest point in Jordan is Jabal Umm ad Dami, reaching an elevation of 1,854 meters (6,083 feet).

Jordan experiences a predominantly arid climate, with hot and dry summers and cool winters. However, there are variations in temperature and precipitation across different regions. The western part of the country, including Amman, has a Mediterranean climate with hot summers and cool, rainy winters. The eastern desert areas, including Wadi Rum, Aqaba, and Petra, have a desert climate, with extremely high temperatures in summer and cooler winters.

Rainfall is scarce throughout most of the country, with the majority of precipitation occurring between November and April. The northern and western regions receive more rainfall compared to the eastern desert areas, which are considerably drier.

The diverse geography and climate of Jordan offer visitors a range of experiences, from exploring ancient ruins in the desert to enjoying the vibrant culture and history of urban areas. Whether it's hiking through nature reserves, floating in the Dead Sea, or discovering the beauty of ancient landscapes, Jordan's geography and climate contribute to its unique allure as a captivating destination.

Brief History

The history of Jordan is a tapestry woven with the threads of ancient civilizations, conquests, and cultural exchanges. The region of modern-day Jordan has been inhabited since prehistoric times, with evidence of early human settlements dating back to the Paleolithic period.

Jordan's historical significance can be traced back to the biblical era, with several notable events occurring within its borders. In the ancient city of Petra, hidden away within the crimson cliffs, the Nabateans, an ingenious people, carved magnificent facades into the rock, creating a thriving trading hub. For centuries, Petra's secrets remained hidden from the world, until an explorer named Johann Ludwig Burckhardt rediscovered its grandeur in 1812.

As time went on, the region witnessed the arrival of the Greeks, who brought their Hellenistic influence to the land. The city of Jerash flourished under their rule, with towering columns, grand theaters, and ornate temples standing as testaments to their civilization.

The Romans, known for their architectural prowess, followed the Greeks, leaving their own majestic footprints on Jordanian soil. Amman, known as Philadelphia in ancient times, became a bustling city adorned with splendid ruins. The towering pillars of the Temple of Hercules and the remarkable amphitheater stand as reminders of Rome's once-great presence.

In the 7th century CE, Islam reached the land, and the Umayyad Caliphate established its capital in the desert oasis of Amman. The city flourished, showcasing the architectural brilliance of Islamic civilization. The Umayyads built the Qasr Al-Kharana fortress and the Qasr Amra palace, where stunning frescoes still adorn the walls.

Jordan's history continued to unfold through the medieval period, witnessing the clashes of the Crusades as European powers sought control over the Holy Land. Castles such as Ajloun Castle and Kerak Castle stood as formidable defenses against invading forces.

In the 20th century, the Hashemite Kingdom of Jordan emerged. Led by King Abdullah I, the country navigated the challenges of the modern era, fostering stability and progress. Jordan became a beacon of peace, serving as a refuge for those displaced by regional conflicts.

In recent times, Jordan has pursued a path of modernization and development, focusing on sectors such as tourism, industry, and technology. It has played a crucial role in regional politics and has actively sought peace and stability in the Middle East.

Today, Jordan stands as a testament to its rich historical legacy, with archaeological sites, ancient ruins, and cultural heritage preserving the stories of the past. The country embraces its history while embracing the challenges and opportunities of the present, offering visitors a chance to immerse themselves in a living timeline of human civilization.

Ancient Legends and Biblical Sites

Jordan is a land steeped in ancient legends and biblical history, with numerous sites of great significance. Here are some notable ancient legends and biblical sites in Jordan:

1. Mount Nebo: According to the Bible, Mount Nebo is where Moses stood and gazed upon the Promised Land before his death. It offers panoramic views of the Jordan Valley, the Dead Sea, and the hills of Jerusalem.

2. Madaba: Known as the "City of Mosaics," Madaba is home to the famous Madaba Map, a Byzantine mosaic that depicts the Holy Land and provides insights into the biblical geography of the region.

3. Petra: While not directly mentioned in the Bible, Petra has captivated the imaginations of people for centuries. Its ancient ruins, including the iconic Treasury, evoke a sense of wonder and mystery.

4. Bethany Beyond the Jordan: Located along the eastern bank of the Jordan River, this biblical site is believed to be the place where John the Baptist baptized Jesus Christ.

5. Amman Citadel: Situated in the heart of Amman, the Amman Citadel has a history dating back thousands of years. It is believed to be the site of the ancient city of Rabbath-Ammon mentioned in the Bible.

6. Umm Qais (Gadara): Mentioned in the New Testament, Umm Qais is believed to be one of the cities where Jesus performed miracles. It offers stunning views of the Sea of Galilee, the Golan Heights, and the Jordan Valley.

7. Lot's Cave (Makawir): According to biblical accounts, this cave is where Lot and his daughters sought refuge after fleeing the destruction of Sodom and Gomorrah. Makawir is a captivating archaeological site with ancient fortifications.

8. Pella: This ancient city is associated with early Christian history and is mentioned in the Bible as a refuge for the early Christians fleeing Jerusalem. It offers well-preserved Roman and Byzantine ruins.

9. Um Al-Rasas: This UNESCO World Heritage site features early Christian ruins, including impressive mosaic floors. It is believed to be the location of the biblical city of Mephaat mentioned in the Book of Jeremiah.

10. Ajloun Castle: Built during the Crusader period, Ajloun Castle played a role in the biblical narrative. It offers a glimpse into the medieval history of the region.

11. Bethabara: Located along the Jordan River, Bethabara is believed to be the place where Jesus was baptized by John the Baptist. It is also associated with the crossing of the Israelites into the Promised Land.

12. Machaerus: This ancient fortress was the site of the execution of John the Baptist. It offers stunning views of the Dead Sea and the surrounding desert.

13. Shobak Castle: Also known as Montreal, Shobak Castle was built by the Crusaders in the 12th century. It played a role in the conflicts between the Crusaders and Saladin, the Muslim leader.

14. Lot's Wife: According to biblical accounts, Lot's wife was turned into a pillar of salt when she looked back at the destruction of Sodom and Gomorrah. It is believed that this event occurred near the Dead Sea, and the pillar of salt is said to be there.

15. Kerak Castle: Another Crusader fortress, Kerak Castle played a significant role in the Crusades. It is perched on a hilltop and offers panoramic views of the surrounding landscape.

16. Al-Maghtas: Also known as Bethany on the Jordan, Al-Maghtas is a UNESCO World Heritage site associated with the baptism of Jesus. It is located on the eastern bank of the Jordan River.

17. Umm Ar-Rasas: This archaeological site is known for its well-preserved Byzantine and early Islamic ruins. It features several churches with intricate mosaic floors, including the Church of Saint Stephen.

18. Tel Mar Elias: Believed to be the burial site of the Prophet Elijah, Tel Mar Elias is a hilltop archaeological site with ancient remains and a small chapel dedicated to Elijah.

19. Mukawir: Mukawir is believed to be the site of the biblical fortress of Machaerus, where John the Baptist was imprisoned and beheaded. The site offers commanding views of the Dead Sea.

20. Ain Ghazal: This archaeological site near Amman reveals the remains of one of the oldest known settlements in the world, dating back to the Neolithic period. It provides insights into the lives of early humans in the region.

These ancient legends and biblical sites add layers of historical and cultural significance to Jordan, showcasing the country's rich heritage and its connections to biblical narratives and ancient civilizations. Exploring these sites will allow you delve into the stories that have shaped this fascinating land.

Chapter 2: Jordan Travel Essentials

As you embark on your journey to the enchanting land of Jordan, it is essential to familiarize yourself with important information that will enhance your travel experience.

Entry Points:
Jordan can be accessed through several entry points. The most common points of entry are Queen Alia International Airport, located near the capital city of Amman, and King Hussein Bridge (Allenby Bridge) on the Jordan-Israel border. Additionally, there are land border crossings with neighboring countries such as Saudi Arabia, Iraq, and Syria.

Transportation Options:
<u>Within Jordan:</u>
Travelers have various transportation options to explore the country. Taxis are readily available in cities and towns, and it is recommended to negotiate fares before the journey. Rental cars can be hired from major cities and airports, but driving in Jordan

may require caution due to local driving habits. Public buses and minibusses (known as service taxis) are economical options for traveling between cities and towns, offering both comfort and affordability.

Reaching Jordan:
By Air:

Queen Alia International Airport serves as the primary gateway to Jordan, with numerous international airlines operating flights to and from major cities worldwide. Amman is well-connected to other regional airports, making it convenient for travelers to reach Jordan by air.

By Land:

If you are traveling overland, Jordan can be reached from neighboring countries. Border crossings are open with Israel, Saudi Arabia, Iraq, and Syria. It is advisable to research the specific border crossing points and their operating hours before planning your journey.

Currency:
The official currency of Jordan is the Jordanian Dinar (JOD). It is recommended to exchange

currency at banks or authorized exchange offices, as they usually offer better rates than hotels or airports. Credit cards are widely accepted in major establishments, but it is advisable to carry cash for smaller vendors and in remote areas.

Time Zone:
Jordan follows Eastern European Time (EET), which is UTC+2 during standard time and UTC+3 during daylight saving time. Jordan does observe daylight saving time, so it is important to check the local time before your visit.

Language Spoken:
The official language of Jordan is Arabic. English is widely spoken and understood, particularly in urban areas, tourist sites, hotels, and restaurants. Travelers will generally find it easy to communicate in English, although learning a few basic Arabic phrases can be helpful and greatly appreciated by locals.

Visa Requirements:
Most travelers to Jordan are required to obtain a visa before arrival. The Jordanian government offers different types of visas, including tourist visas,

business visas, and transit visas. It is advisable to check the nearest Jordanian embassy or consulate for the most up-to-date information regarding visa requirements based on your nationality and purpose of travel.

Here are some types of Visas you may need to get when traveling to Jordan depending on the purpose of your travel:

1. Tourist Visa: The tourist visa is the most common type of visa for travelers visiting Jordan for tourism purposes. It allows visitors to explore the country's attractions, historical sites, and natural wonders. Tourist visas can be obtained in advance from Jordanian embassies or consulates in your home country or upon arrival at designated entry points such as Queen Alia International Airport or select land border crossings. The visa is typically valid for a single entry and permits a stay of up to 30 days, with the option to extend if needed.

2. Multiple Entry Visa: The multiple entry visa is suitable for travelers planning to enter and exit Jordan multiple times during their trip. This type of visa provides flexibility in crossing borders without the need to obtain a new visa for each entry. It is particularly useful for individuals who wish to explore neighboring countries and return to Jordan during their itinerary. The multiple entry visa can be obtained from Jordanian embassies or consulates before traveling to Jordan.

3. Business Visa: Travelers visiting Jordan for business-related purposes, such as attending conferences, meetings, or exploring potential business opportunities, may need to obtain a business visa. This type of visa typically requires sponsorship from a Jordanian company or organization. The sponsoring entity will provide necessary documents, such as an invitation letter, to support the visa application. Business visas may have specific validity periods depending on the nature of the visit.

4. Work Visa: Individuals seeking employment in Jordan must obtain a work visa in addition to a work permit. The work visa is usually sponsored by a Jordanian employer who has obtained the necessary approvals from the Ministry of Labor. Work visas are issued for specific employment contracts and are subject to renewal upon expiration.

5. Student Visa: Students planning to study in Jordan should apply for a student visa. The visa application process typically involves providing proof of enrollment in an accredited educational institution in Jordan, along with other required documents. Student visas are usually issued for the duration of the study program.

6. Transit Visa: If you have a layover in Jordan and plan to stay in the country for a short period, you may be eligible for a transit visa. This type of visa allows you to stay in Jordan for a limited duration while in transit to another destination. Transit visas are usually valid for up to 7 days.

7. Diplomatic and Official Visas: Diplomatic and official visas are issued to individuals traveling to Jordan on official government business or representing their respective governments. These visas are granted based on diplomatic agreements and protocols between Jordan and the visitor's home country. The application process for diplomatic and official visas involves coordination between the relevant government agencies and diplomatic missions.

8. Temporary Residence Visa: Temporary residence visas are issued to individuals who intend to stay in Jordan for an extended period for purposes such as work, study, or family reunification. These visas are typically obtained through sponsorship by a Jordanian individual, company, or educational institution. Temporary residence visas allow for a longer stay in Jordan and may require additional documentation, such as proof of accommodation, financial means, or educational enrollment.

9. Humanitarian Visa: Humanitarian visas are granted to individuals traveling to Jordan for humanitarian purposes, such as participating in relief efforts, volunteering with humanitarian organizations, or conducting research related to humanitarian issues. These visas may have specific requirements and may require sponsorship or coordination with relevant Jordanian authorities or organizations.

10. Medical Treatment Visa: If you are seeking medical treatment in Jordan, you may need to apply for a medical treatment visa. These visas are issued to individuals traveling to Jordan for medical purposes, including consultations, surgeries, or specialized treatments. Medical treatment visas may require supporting documentation from recognized medical institutions or healthcare providers in Jordan.

11. Journalist Visa: Journalists and media professionals planning to visit Jordan for journalistic activities, such as reporting, filming, or conducting interviews, may need to obtain a journalist visa. This type of visa may require accreditation from the Jordanian government or relevant media organizations.

12. Investor Visa: Individuals planning to invest in Jordan or establish a business in the country may be eligible for an investor visa. These visas are granted to foreign investors who meet specific investment criteria set by the Jordanian government. The application process for an investor visa usually involves providing detailed business plans, financial information, and evidence of investment intentions.

13. Retirement Visa: Jordan offers a retirement residency program that allows foreign retirees to live in the country. The retirement visa requires applicants to meet certain criteria, such as a minimum age, proof of financial stability, and health insurance coverage. This visa option is designed to attract retirees who wish to enjoy their retirement years in Jordan.

It is important to note that the specific requirements, documentation, and application processes for each type of visa can vary. It is recommended to consult with the nearest Jordanian embassy or consulate or refer to official government sources for the most accurate and up-to-date information regarding the visa type that best suits your travel purpose.

Visa Application Process: If you are required to obtain a visa in advance, you will need to submit the necessary documents to the nearest Jordanian embassy or consulate. The application process typically involves completing a visa application form, providing a valid passport with at least six months of validity remaining, passport-sized photographs, proof of travel arrangements (such as flight tickets), proof of accommodation in Jordan, and evidence of sufficient funds to cover your stay. It is advisable to apply for the visa well in advance of your intended travel dates to allow for processing time.

Visa Fees: Visa fees vary depending on the type and duration of the visa. The fees are usually payable in local currency or sometimes in US dollars. It is recommended to check the current visa fees with the embassy or consulate before submitting your application. Additionally, keep in mind that visa fees are generally non-refundable, even if the visa application is denied.

Border Crossings: If you plan to enter Jordan by land, it is important to research the available border crossing points and their operating hours. Some border crossings have specific entry requirements, and not all are open to all nationalities. For example, the border crossing between Jordan and Israel (King Hussein Bridge/Allenby Bridge) is only accessible to certain nationalities and requires pre-arranged permits. It is advisable to check the latest information and requirements for each border crossing to ensure a smooth entry into Jordan.

Visa on Arrival: Visitors from many countries are eligible for a visa on arrival, which allows them to obtain a tourist visa upon reaching Jordan. The visa on arrival is usually valid for a stay of up to 30 days, but it is advisable to check the latest regulations as they can be subject to change. The visa fee can be paid in cash or by credit card at the immigration counter.

Visa Extensions: If you wish to extend your stay in Jordan beyond the initial visa validity period, it is possible to apply for an extension at the nearest Jordanian immigration office. Extensions are granted based on the discretion of the immigration authorities and require valid reasons for the request.

Visa Exemptions: Some nationalities are exempt from obtaining a visa to enter Jordan for a certain period. These exemptions vary depending on bilateral agreements and diplomatic relations between Jordan and specific countries. For example, citizens of certain countries such as the United States, United Kingdom, Canada, Australia, and many European Union nations are granted a visa-free stay for a specified duration, usually ranging from 14 to 90 days. However, it is crucial to verify the duration and conditions of visa exemptions based on your nationality before traveling to Jordan.

Overstaying and Penalties: It is important to adhere to the visa regulations and not overstay your permitted duration in Jordan. Overstaying can result in fines, deportation, and difficulties when reentering the country in the future. If you need to extend your stay beyond the visa's validity, it is advisable to apply for a visa extension before your current visa expires.

Visa Requirements for Bordering Countries: If you plan to travel to Jordan through its land border crossings with neighboring countries such as Israel, Saudi Arabia, Iraq, or Syria, it is important to understand the specific visa requirements for each border. Some border crossings may require pre-approved visas or permits, while others may grant visas on arrival. Research and confirm the visa requirements for each border crossing, especially if you intend to visit multiple countries during your trip.

Visa Validity and Duration of Stay: The validity and duration of stay permitted on a tourist visa may vary depending on the type of visa obtained. Typically, tourist visas are valid for a single-entry stay of 30 days, but it is advisable to check the specific validity and duration details based on your visa type and nationality. If you wish to stay longer in Jordan, you may need to apply for a visa extension before your current visa expires.

Visa Sponsorship: In some cases, individuals visiting Jordan for purposes such as family visits or conferences may require a visa sponsorship from a Jordanian resident or organization. The sponsoring party will need to provide the necessary documents to support the visa application, such as a letter of invitation, proof of relationship, or event registration details.

Health Insurance: While not directly related to visa requirements, it is highly recommended to have comprehensive travel health insurance that covers medical emergencies and repatriation. Some countries may require proof of health insurance coverage upon visa application or entry into Jordan. Ensure that your insurance policy is valid for the entire duration of your stay and provides adequate coverage for your needs.

Exit Fees: Upon departing Jordan, there may be an exit fee payable at the airport or land border. This fee is typically included in the price of your airline ticket, but it is advisable to confirm whether any additional fees apply and have sufficient cash or currency available, if necessary.

Volunteer and Humanitarian Work: If you intend to engage in volunteer or humanitarian work in Jordan, it is important to ensure compliance with local regulations. Depending on the nature and duration of the work, you may need to obtain specific visas or permits, such as a volunteer visa or a permit from the Ministry of Social Development. It is advisable to consult with relevant organizations or the nearest Jordanian embassy or consulate for guidance on the appropriate visa requirements.

Visa-Free Zones: Jordan has designated visa-free zones, including the Aqaba Special Economic Zone (ASEZ). Travelers entering Aqaba through its designated entry points, such as Aqaba Airport or the Wadi Araba border crossing with Israel, can enjoy visa-free access for stays of up to 30 days. This provision allows visitors to explore the Red Sea coastal area, including Aqaba, without obtaining a separate visa. However, if you plan to travel outside the ASEZ, you will need to obtain the appropriate visa for Jordan.

Visa-on-Arrival Fees: If you are eligible for a visa on arrival, it is important to note that there is a fee associated with obtaining the visa. The visa-on-arrival fee can be paid in cash or by credit card at the immigration counter. It is advisable to have the exact amount in local currency or carry sufficient funds in case credit card payments are not accepted.

Passport Validity: Ensure that your passport has a validity of at least six months beyond your intended departure date from Jordan. Some airlines and immigration authorities may deny boarding or entry if your passport does not meet the required validity criteria.

Other important information to note to enhance your stay in Jordan include:

Restricted Areas: Certain areas in Jordan, such as the Jordan-Syria border region, may have restricted access or require special permits due to security concerns. It is important to stay informed about any travel advisories or restrictions issued by your home country's government and the Jordanian authorities.

Travel Registration: While not mandatory, it is recommended to register your travel plans with your embassy or consulate before visiting Jordan. This enables your home country's diplomatic mission to provide assistance or contact you in case of emergencies or unforeseen circumstances during your stay.

COVID-19 Travel Requirements: Due to the ongoing COVID-19 pandemic, travel requirements and restrictions may be in place. This includes mandatory COVID-19 testing, health declarations, and quarantine measures. Stay updated on the latest travel advisories and entry requirements related to COVID-19 by checking official government sources and contacting your airline or tour operator.

Prohibited Items: Familiarize yourself with the list of prohibited items and substances that are not allowed to be brought into Jordan. This includes narcotics, firearms, and certain medications.

Violation of these regulations can lead to serious legal consequences.

Respect for Local Customs: Jordan is a predominantly Muslim country, and it is important to respect local customs and traditions. Dress modestly, particularly when visiting religious sites, and adhere to local norms and etiquettes. Public displays of affection and consumption of alcohol in public places may be considered inappropriate or offensive.

Safety and Security: Jordan is generally considered safe for travelers, but it is always advisable to take common safety precautions. Be vigilant, particularly in crowded areas and tourist sites, and keep your belongings secure. It is recommended to follow any travel advisories issued by your home country and stay informed about the local security situation.

Consular Assistance: Familiarize yourself with the contact details and location of your country's embassy or consulate in Jordan. In case of emergencies, such as lost or stolen passports, accidents, or legal issues, contact your embassy or consulate for consular assistance and guidance.

Travel Insurance: It is highly recommended to obtain comprehensive travel insurance that covers medical expenses, trip cancellation or interruption, lost or stolen belongings, and emergency medical evacuation. Review the policy carefully to ensure it meets your needs and provides adequate coverage for your entire stay in Jordan.

Health and Vaccinations: Check if any specific vaccinations are recommended or required before traveling to Jordan. It is advisable to consult with your healthcare provider or a travel health clinic at least a few weeks before your departure to ensure you are up to date with routine vaccinations and any necessary additional immunizations.

Local Laws and Regulations: Familiarize yourself with the local laws and regulations of Jordan to avoid any inadvertent violations. Respect cultural sensitivities, religious customs, and social norms. Be aware that penalties for drug offenses, including possession and trafficking, can be severe.

Driving in Jordan: If you plan to drive in Jordan, familiarize yourself with local traffic laws and regulations. International driving permits are generally required, and it is advisable to have adequate insurance coverage. Be cautious on the roads, as driving habits and road conditions may differ from what you are accustomed to.

Internet and Communication: Jordan has a well-developed telecommunications infrastructure, and mobile phone coverage is widely available. Consider obtaining a local SIM card or using international roaming services to stay connected during your stay. Wi-Fi is also accessible in hotels, restaurants, and many public areas.

Climate and Seasonal Considerations: Jordan experiences a wide range of climates, from hot desert summers to cooler temperatures in the highlands. Consider the weather conditions and pack accordingly, including appropriate clothing, sunscreen, and other essentials. Be prepared for temperature variations, especially if you plan to visit different regions of the country.

Cultural Etiquette: Embrace the cultural diversity of Jordan by respecting local customs and traditions. It is customary to greet people with a handshake, and it is polite to use your right hand for gestures and while eating. Remove your shoes when entering mosques or private homes, and be mindful of local sensitivities when taking photographs, particularly of people.

Tipping and Bargaining: Tipping is common in Jordan, especially in restaurants, hotels, and for service providers. It is customary to leave a gratuity of around 10% of the total bill. Bargaining is also a common practice in markets and souks, so feel free to negotiate prices when shopping for souvenirs or goods.

Remember to stay informed and updated on any travel advisories, local customs, and current events in Jordan. By considering these additional aspects, you can ensure a well-informed and prepared journey to Jordan. Enjoy the diverse landscapes, historical treasures, and warm hospitality that await you in this captivating country.

Chapter 3: Planning Your Itinerary

Here are sample itineraries for different durations of stay in Jordan:

3-Day Itinerary:

Day 1: Amman and Jerash

- Explore the capital city of Amman, visiting highlights such as the Roman Theater, Citadel, and King Abdullah Mosque.
- Take a day trip to Jerash, one of the best-preserved Roman cities in the world, known for its impressive ruins and ancient architecture.

Day 2: Petra

- Travel to Petra, a UNESCO World Heritage Site and one of the New Seven Wonders of the World.
- Spend the day exploring the iconic Treasury, the Monastery, the Royal Tombs, and other remarkable rock-cut structures.

Day 3: Wadi Rum and Aqaba

- Embark on a desert adventure in Wadi Rum, known for its stunning landscapes and sandstone mountains.
- Enjoy a 4x4 jeep tour, camel ride, or hot air balloon ride to experience the beauty of the desert.
- Head to Aqaba, a coastal city on the Red Sea, and relax on the beaches, go snorkeling or diving in the vibrant coral reefs.

7-Day Itinerary:

Day 1-2: Amman and Jerash

- Explore Amman's cultural and historical sites, including the Roman Theater, Citadel, and Rainbow Street.
- Visit Jerash to immerse yourself in the ancient Roman ruins and marvel at the well-preserved architecture.

Day 3-4: Petra and Wadi Rum

- Spend a full day exploring Petra, walking through the Siq, discovering the Treasury, and exploring the various tombs and temples.

- Journey to Wadi Rum for a memorable desert experience, enjoying jeep safaris, camel rides, and stargazing.

Day 5-6: Dead Sea and Madaba
- Relax and float in the buoyant waters of the Dead Sea, known for its therapeutic properties.
- Visit the biblical city of Madaba to see the famous mosaic map of the Holy Land and explore Byzantine-era churches.

Day 7: Aqaba
- Enjoy the beach resorts and vibrant underwater life of Aqaba.
- Engage in water activities like snorkeling or diving, or simply unwind on the sandy shores.

10-Day Itinerary:

Day 1-2: Amman and Jerash
- Spend time in Amman, exploring its vibrant markets, cafes, and museums.
- Visit the ancient city of Jerash and immerse yourself in its rich Roman history.

Day 3-4: Petra and Wadi Rum

- Explore the hidden city of Petra, uncovering its intricate rock-carved architecture and hiking through the scenic landscapes.
- Experience the vast beauty of Wadi Rum with desert safaris, camping under the stars, and enjoying traditional Bedouin hospitality.

Day 5-6: Dana Biosphere Reserve and Shobak Castle

- Venture to the Dana Biosphere Reserve, a nature reserve with stunning landscapes, diverse wildlife, and hiking trails.
- Visit Shobak Castle, a Crusader fortress perched on a hilltop, and admire its historical significance and panoramic views.

Day 7-8: Dead Sea and Ma'in Hot Springs

- Relax and float in the therapeutic waters of the Dead Sea.
- Visit the Ma'in Hot Springs and indulge in the natural hot springs and waterfalls.

Day 9-10: Aqaba and Red Sea

- Head to Aqaba for beach relaxation, water sports, and coral reef exploration.
- Take a boat trip for snorkeling or diving in the Red Sea to witness its abundant marine life.

14-Day Itinerary:

Day 1-2: Amman and Jerash
- Explore the capital city of Amman, visiting landmarks like the Roman Theater, Citadel, and the bustling downtown area.
- Take a day trip to Jerash to discover its well-preserved Roman ruins and ancient city streets.

Day 3-4: Petra
- Spend two full days exploring the magnificent archaeological site of Petra, including the Treasury, Monastery, and High Place of Sacrifice.
- Consider taking a guided tour to learn about the history and significance of this UNESCO World Heritage Site.

Day 5-6: Wadi Rum
- Venture into the stunning desert landscapes of Wadi Rum.

- Enjoy jeep safaris, camel rides, and overnight camping experiences to fully immerse yourself in the beauty of this vast desert.

Day 7-8: Aqaba and Red Sea

- Head to the coastal city of Aqaba and indulge in water activities like snorkeling, scuba diving, or sailing in the Red Sea.
- Relax on the beaches or explore the vibrant marine life with a glass-bottom boat tour or a visit to the Aqaba Marine Park.

Day 9-11: Dead Sea, Madaba, and Mount Nebo

- Experience the unique sensation of floating in the mineral-rich waters of the Dead Sea.
- Visit the town of Madaba, known for its Byzantine-era mosaics, including the famous Madaba Map.
- Take a trip to Mount Nebo to enjoy panoramic views of the Jordan Valley and the Promised Land.

Day 12-14: Northern Jordan and Ajloun

- Explore the ancient city of Umm Qais (Gadara), known for its Greco-Roman ruins and panoramic views of the Sea of Galilee.

- Visit the impressive Ajloun Castle, a 12th-century fortress situated on a hilltop.
- Discover the natural beauty of the northern region, including the lush green landscapes of the Jordan Valley and the beautiful waterfalls of Wadi Mujib.

21-Day Itinerary:

Day 1-4: Amman and Surroundings
- Spend a few days exploring Amman and its surroundings, including the ancient Citadel, Roman Theater, and the lively markets of downtown.
- Visit the Desert Castles in the eastern desert, such as Qasr Amra and Qasr Azraq, known for their unique architecture and historical significance.

Day 5-8: Petra and Wadi Rum
- Dedicate ample time to fully explore the wonders of Petra, including lesser-known sites like the High Place of Sacrifice and the Royal Tombs.
- Immerse yourself in the captivating landscapes of Wadi Rum, enjoying camel treks, sandboarding, and peaceful nights under the starry desert sky.

Day 9-12: Dead Sea, Madaba, and Mount Nebo

- Relax and rejuvenate at the Dead Sea, taking advantage of the unique healing properties of its mineral-rich waters.
- Visit the biblical town of Madaba to see the famous mosaic map of the Holy Land and explore its Byzantine-era churches.
- Venture to Mount Nebo for breathtaking views and a glimpse of the revered site where Moses is said to have seen the Promised Land.

Day 13-16: Northern Jordan and Jerash

- Explore the lush green landscapes of the Jordan Valley, including the stunning landscapes of Wadi Mujib and the biblical sites of Bethany Beyond the Jordan.
- Spend a day discovering the Roman ruins of Jerash, immersing yourself in its well-preserved architecture and vibrant history.

Day 17-19: Dana Biosphere Reserve and Shobak Castle

- Venture into the beautiful Dana Biosphere Reserve, a haven for nature lovers and hikers, with its diverse wildlife and picturesque landscapes.
- Visit Shobak Castle, an impressive Crusader fortress perched on a hilltop, and explore its historical ruins and panoramic views.

Day 20-21: Ajloun and Umm Qais
- Journey to the Ajloun region and explore the imposing Ajloun Castle, known for its strategic location and fascinating history.
- Visit the ancient city of Umm Qais (Gadara) and walk among its well-preserved Roman ruins while enjoying breathtaking views of the Sea of Galilee and the Golan Heights.

This 21-day itinerary provides a comprehensive experience of Jordan's diverse landscapes, historical sites, and cultural heritage. You can adjust the itinerary based on your preferences and allocate more time to specific locations or activities that interest you the most.

Remember to consider travel times and distances between destinations, as well as the operating hours of attractions and sites, when planning your itinerary.

Chapter 4: Where to Stay

Here are various accommodation options available in different cities and regions of Jordan, ranging from luxury hotels to budget-friendly guesthouses and campsites:

1. Amman:
- Luxury Hotels: The St. Regis Amman, Four Seasons Hotel Amman, InterContinental Amman.
- Mid-range Hotels: Amman Marriott Hotel, Grand Millennium Hotel, Amman Rotana.
- Budget-Friendly Options: Jordan Tower Hotel, Sydney Hotel, Arab Tower Hotel.

2. Petra:
- Luxury Hotels: Mövenpick Resort Petra, Petra Marriott Hotel, Old Village Resort.
- Mid-range Hotels: Petra Guest House Hotel, Seven Wonders Hotel, Al Rashid Hotel.
- Budget-Friendly Options: Rocky Mountain Hotel, Candles Hotel, Tetra Tree Hotel.

3. Wadi Rum:

- Luxury Desert Camps: Sun City Camp, Wadi Rum Night Luxury Camp, Memories Aicha Luxury Camp.
- Mid-range Desert Camps: Rahayeb Desert Camp, Hasan Zawaideh Camp, Wadi Rum Nature Camp.
- Budget-Friendly Desert Camps: Bedouin Lifestyle Camp, Captain's Desert Camp, Rum Stars Camp.

4. Aqaba:
- Luxury Hotels: Kempinski Hotel Aqaba, Mövenpick Resort & Residences Aqaba, InterContinental Aqaba.
- Mid-range Hotels: Marina Plaza Hotel, DoubleTree by Hilton Hotel Aqaba, Golden Tulip Aqaba.
- Budget-Friendly Options: Dweik Hotel 3, Aqaba Adventure Divers Resort, Al Qidra Hotel & Suites.

5. Dead Sea:
- Luxury Hotels: Kempinski Hotel Ishtar Dead Sea, Mövenpick Resort & Spa Dead Sea, Hilton Dead Sea Resort & Spa.
- Mid-range Hotels: Crowne Plaza Jordan Dead Sea Resort & Spa, Dead Sea Spa Hotel, Ramada Resort Dead Sea.

- Budget-Friendly Options: Ramada Resort by Wyndham Dead Sea, Dead Sea Sun Hotel, Dead Sea Marriott Resort.

6. Dana Biosphere Reserve:
- Feynan Ecolodge: A unique and award-winning eco-friendly lodge offering an authentic experience in the heart of the reserve.
- Dana Tower Hotel: A cozy hotel located in the village of Dana, offering comfortable accommodation and stunning views.
- Rummana Campsite: A basic campsite within the reserve, perfect for those seeking a rustic camping experience in nature.

7. Madaba:
- Madaba Hotel: A well-known hotel located in the heart of Madaba, offering comfortable rooms and a central location.
- Mariam Hotel: A budget-friendly option with clean and basic rooms, ideal for travelers on a budget.
- Saint John Hotel: A mid-range hotel situated near the St. George Church, known for its friendly staff and convenient location.

8. Jerash:

- Olive Branch Hotel: A cozy hotel located near the Jerash ruins, offering comfortable rooms and a friendly atmosphere.
- Jarash Inn Hotel: A mid-range hotel with spacious rooms and a rooftop terrace offering panoramic views of the city.
- Beit Al Baraka: A guesthouse located in the heart of Jerash, offering traditional-style rooms and a tranquil courtyard.

9. Ajloun:

- Ajloun Hotel: A budget-friendly hotel located in the center of Ajloun town, offering basic rooms and easy access to Ajloun Castle.
- Ajloun Forest Reserve Cabins: Rustic cabins situated within the Ajloun Forest Reserve, perfect for nature lovers and hikers.

10. Umm Qais:

- Umm Qais Resthouse: A simple guesthouse offering comfortable rooms and stunning views of the surrounding countryside.
- Beit Al Baraka Umm Qais: A guesthouse located in a renovated historic building, providing a unique and charming experience.

11. Ma'in Hot Springs:

- Evason Ma'in Hot Springs: A luxury resort nestled in a breathtaking valley, offering hot spring pools and spa facilities.
- Ma'in Hot Springs Hotel: A mid-range hotel overlooking the hot springs, providing comfortable rooms and access to the natural thermal waters.

12. Karak:

- Kerak Castle Hotel: A hotel located near Karak Castle, offering spacious rooms and a rooftop terrace with panoramic views.
- Al Qasr Metropole Hotel: A mid-range hotel situated in the heart of Karak, providing comfortable accommodation and convenient access to local attractions.

13. Dead Sea Resorts:

- The Jordan Valley Marriott Dead Sea Resort & Spa: A luxury resort offering private beach access, spa facilities, and multiple swimming pools.
- Holiday Inn Resort Dead Sea: A mid-range resort with comfortable rooms, a private beach, and family-friendly amenities.

14. Desert Camps in Various Locations:
- Luxury and Mid-range Camps: There are several luxury and mid-range desert camps available in different regions, such as Wadi Rum, offering comfortable accommodation, traditional Bedouin hospitality, and various desert activities.
- Budget-Friendly Camps: There are also budget-friendly campsites and basic Bedouin tents available in Wadi Rum, allowing travelers to experience the desert on a more affordable budget.

These accommodation options offer a range of choices to suit different preferences and budgets. It's always recommended to check reviews, amenities, and location details when making a booking to ensure the accommodation meets your specific needs.

Chapter 5: Amman and Jerash

Amman

Amman, the capital city of Jordan, is a vibrant metropolis with a rich history that dates back several millennia. The city has been inhabited since the Neolithic period and has been influenced by various civilizations, including the Greeks, Romans, Byzantines, and Ottomans. Amman's historical significance lies in its strategic location along ancient trade routes and its role as a crossroads of cultures.

Amman is a dynamic city that seamlessly blends modernity with its historical roots. Here are some key aspects to consider when exploring Amman:

1. Citadel (Jabal al-Qal'a): The Citadel is a historic hilltop site that offers panoramic views of Amman. It showcases ruins from different periods, including the Temple of Hercules, the Umayyad Palace, and the Byzantine Church. It's a fascinating place to explore and understand the layers of history that have shaped the city.

2. Roman Theater: The Roman Theater is one of Amman's iconic landmarks. Built during the 2nd century AD, it could seat around 6,000 spectators. Today, it serves as a venue for cultural events and festivals. Climbing to the top offers a fantastic view of downtown Amman.

3. Rainbow Street: Rainbow Street is a vibrant and bustling thoroughfare in the heart of Amman. It is known for its trendy cafes, art galleries, boutique shops, and lively atmosphere. Taking a stroll along Rainbow Street provides a glimpse into the city's modern culture and offers opportunities for shopping and dining.

4. Amman Citadel Archaeological Museum: Located within the Citadel, the Archaeological Museum houses a collection of artifacts that trace the history of Jordan, from prehistoric times to the Islamic era. The exhibits provide insights into the region's ancient civilizations and cultural heritage.

5. Souk Jara: If you're looking for a unique shopping experience, visit Souk Jara. It is a seasonal open-air market held in the summer months, where local artisans and vendors showcase their handmade crafts, traditional foods, and local products. It's an excellent place to buy souvenirs and immerse yourself in the local atmosphere.

6. Modern Amman: Amman is a modern city with a thriving culinary scene, luxury hotels, and contemporary architecture. Areas like Abdoun, Shmeisani, and Al-Abdali offer upscale shopping centers, high-end restaurants, and entertainment venues.

Entry Fees and Permits:
Many of the attractions in Amman, such as the Citadel and Roman Theater, require an entry fee. The fees vary depending on the attraction and your nationality. It is advisable to check with official sources or local authorities for the most up-to-date entry fees.

Local Guides:
While exploring Amman on your own is possible, hiring a local guide can enhance your experience by providing historical and cultural insights, navigating the city efficiently, and ensuring that you don't miss any important landmarks or hidden gems.

Amman is a city of contrasts, where ancient ruins coexist with modern developments, offering a captivating blend of history, culture, and contemporary experiences. It is a must-visit destination for travelers seeking to explore Jordan's vibrant capital.

Jerash

Jerash, located in northern Jordan, is an ancient city with a rich history dating back to the Roman period. Known as Gerasa in ancient times, Jerash was a prominent city of the Decapolis, a league of ten cities within the Roman Empire. It flourished during the 1st century AD and was an important center of trade, commerce, and culture.

Jerash is widely regarded as one of the best-preserved Greco-Roman cities in the world. Its well-preserved ruins provide a remarkable glimpse into the grandeur and splendor of the ancient Roman civilization. The city's archaeological sites showcase a harmonious blend of Roman, Byzantine, and Umayyad influences.

When visiting Jerash, there are several key sites that you shouldn't miss:

1. Oval Plaza: The Oval Plaza is a spacious public square at the heart of the ancient city. It was the focal point for various social and cultural activities during its prime. The plaza is surrounded by impressive colonnades and important structures such as the Nymphaeum and the Temple of Artemis.

2. Hadrian's Arch: This iconic monumental arch was built to honor Emperor Hadrian's visit to Jerash in the 2nd century AD. It stands as a grand entrance to the city and is a popular spot for photography.

3. Hippodrome: The Hippodrome was an arena for chariot races and other sporting events in ancient times. It is one of the largest and best-preserved hippodromes in the Roman world, offering a glimpse into the entertainment culture of the period.

4. South Theater: The South Theater is an impressive Roman theater that could accommodate around 3,000 spectators. It was primarily used for theatrical performances and still hosts cultural events and concerts today.

5. North Theater: The North Theater is a smaller theater that was mainly used for more intimate performances, including poetry recitals and music. Its well-preserved stage and seating area provide an excellent understanding of ancient theater architecture.

Entry Fees and Permits:
To enter Jerash, visitors need to purchase an entry ticket. The entry fee for Jerash varies depending on the nationality and type of visit. It is advisable to check with official sources or local authorities for the most up-to-date entry fees.

Guided Tours and Local Guides:
Exploring Jerash with a knowledgeable guide can greatly enhance your experience. Local guides are well-versed in the history and significance of the city. They can provide valuable insights, share captivating stories, and bring the ancient ruins to life. They can also help you navigate the site efficiently and ensure that you don't miss any important details.

Visiting Tips:

- Comfortable footwear is recommended as the archaeological site is extensive, and you'll be walking on uneven surfaces.
- It's advisable to carry water, sunscreen, and a hat, especially during the summer months, as the site can be hot and exposed to the sun.
- Visit early in the morning or late in the afternoon to avoid the peak heat and crowds.

Jerash's remarkably preserved ruins and its cultural and historical significance make it a must-visit destination for history enthusiasts and travelers seeking to delve into the grandeur of the ancient Roman Empire.

Chapter 6: Petra and Wadi Rum

Petra

Petra, also known as the "Rose City," is an ancient Nabataean city that flourished from the 4th century BC to the 1st century AD. It was a significant trading hub and a key stop on the caravan routes connecting the Arabian Peninsula, Egypt, and the Mediterranean.

Petra's significance lies in its remarkable rock-cut architecture and its historical and cultural importance. The city is famous for its intricate facades carved into the rose-colored sandstone cliffs, which create a truly awe-inspiring sight. The most iconic structure is Al-Khazneh (The Treasury), which serves as a symbol of Petra. However, there are numerous other structures, including tombs, temples, and ceremonial buildings, that showcase the city's grandeur.

Exploring Petra:

Upon entering Petra, visitors pass through the Siq, a narrow gorge with towering cliffs that provides a dramatic entryway to the city. As you emerge from the Siq, the sight of the Treasury comes into view, leaving visitors in awe of its grandeur. From there, you can continue to explore the main archaeological site, which covers a vast area.

Some notable highlights within Petra include the Street of Facades, the Royal Tombs, the Theater, the Great Temple, and the Monastery (Ad-Deir). Each structure offers unique architectural features and historical significance.

It's important to allocate enough time to fully explore Petra as it is a large site with many attractions. A minimum of one full day is recommended, but if time allows, two or three days would be ideal to fully appreciate its beauty and explore the lesser-known areas.

Entry Fees and Permits:
To enter Petra, visitors need to purchase an entry ticket. The entry fee for Petra varies depending on the duration of your visit. It ranges from 50 JOD (Jordanian Dinar) for a one-day ticket to 90 JOD for

a three-day ticket. Two-day and night entry options are also available. It's advisable to check official sources or with local authorities for the most up-to-date entry fees.

The entry ticket serves as your permit to access Petra. Make sure to keep it with you throughout your visit, as it may be checked at various checkpoints within the site.

Guided Tours and Local Guides:
While exploring Petra on your own is possible, hiring a local guide can greatly enhance your experience. Local guides are knowledgeable about the history, significance, and hidden gems of Petra. They can provide valuable insights, share fascinating stories, and ensure you don't miss any important details. Their expertise can enrich your visit and make it even more memorable.

Petra is an extraordinary archaeological site, filled with history, breathtaking architecture, and natural beauty. It is a UNESCO World Heritage site and one of the New Seven Wonders of the World. Visiting Petra is like stepping back in time, and it is truly a destination that should not be missed when exploring Jordan.

Wadi Rum

Wadi Rum, also known as the Valley of the Moon, is a desert valley located in southern Jordan. It is situated approximately 60 kilometers east of Aqaba. The area spans around 720 square kilometers and is characterized by its unique rock formations, vast sand dunes, and breathtaking landscapes.

Wadi Rum's natural beauty is awe-inspiring. The landscape is dominated by towering sandstone and granite rock formations, some reaching heights of over 1,000 meters. The colors of the rocks vary from red to orange and even shades of pink, creating a surreal and picturesque setting. The desert is also home to narrow canyons, hidden water springs, and ancient inscriptions, adding to its mystique.

Wadi Rum is inhabited by the Bedouin people, who have called this desert home for centuries. The Bedouins are known for their hospitality and their deep connection to the desert. Visiting Wadi Rum provides an opportunity to learn about their rich cultural heritage, traditions, and way of life. Bedouin camps offer a chance to experience their warm hospitality, enjoy traditional meals, and even spend a night under the stars in a Bedouin-style tent.

Wadi Rum offers a captivating blend of natural wonders, cultural experiences, and adventurous activities, making it an unforgettable destination for travelers seeking to immerse themselves in the splendor of Jordan's desert.

Activities and Attractions:
Wadi Rum's breathtaking landscapes, unique rock formations, and cultural heritage make it a popular destination for various activities and attractions.
Exploring Wadi Rum offers a range of activities and attractions:

Jeep Tours: One of the most popular ways to explore Wadi Rum is by taking a 4x4 jeep tour. Local Bedouin guides drive visitors through the desert, taking them to iconic sites, such as Lawrence's Spring, Khazali Canyon, and the Seven Pillars of Wisdom. The tours usually include stops for breathtaking viewpoints, sand dune climbing, and visits to ancient rock inscriptions.

Camel Rides: Another traditional way to experience Wadi Rum is by riding a camel. This slow-paced journey allows you to appreciate the tranquility of the desert and enjoy the rhythmic motion of these magnificent animals. Bedouin guides lead the camel rides, sharing stories and insights along the way.

Hiking and Trekking: Wadi Rum offers fantastic opportunities for hiking and trekking enthusiasts. Exploring the canyons, scaling the rocks, and hiking up sand dunes provide an up-close encounter with the desert's natural beauty. Trekking routes can vary in difficulty, catering to different skill levels and interests.

Hot Air Balloon Rides: For a truly memorable experience, consider taking a hot air balloon ride over Wadi Rum. Floating above the desert, you'll enjoy panoramic views of the stunning landscapes, capturing the vastness and grandeur of the valley from a unique perspective.

Sunset and Sunrise: Witnessing the sunrise or sunset in Wadi Rum is a truly magical experience. The shifting colors of the desert as the sun rises or sets create a mesmerizing display of light and shadow. Many tours and camps organize special excursions to viewpoints where you can capture the beauty of these moments and create lasting memories.

Rock Climbing: Wadi Rum is a paradise for rock climbers of all levels. The challenging cliffs and rock formations offer numerous routes for climbers to test their skills and enjoy the thrill of scaling the desert walls. Whether you are a beginner or an experienced climber, there are options available to suit your abilities and preferences.

Traditional Bedouin Meals: When visiting Wadi Rum, be sure to savor the traditional Bedouin cuisine. Many camps offer delicious meals prepared with local ingredients and cooking methods. From zarb (a traditional Bedouin barbecue cooked in an underground sand oven) to mansaf (a signature Jordanian dish), you can enjoy a taste of authentic Bedouin flavors while surrounded by the desert's tranquility.

Film Locations: Wadi Rum's otherworldly landscapes have attracted filmmakers from around the world. It has served as a backdrop for several renowned movies, including "Lawrence of Arabia" and "The Martian." Film enthusiasts can explore specific filming locations and relive memorable scenes against the backdrop of this extraordinary desert.

Conservation and Sustainability: Wadi Rum is committed to preserving its natural beauty and cultural heritage. Efforts are made to promote sustainable tourism practices, protect the environment, and support the local Bedouin community. As a responsible visitor, it is essential to respect the guidelines, leave no trace, and support local initiatives that contribute to the conservation of this unique ecosystem.

Camping and Stargazing:
Spending a night in Wadi Rum is an extraordinary experience. Bedouin-style camps offer comfortable accommodations in traditional tents, allowing visitors to immerse themselves in the desert ambiance. As night falls, Wadi Rum's dark skies provide an ideal setting for stargazing. The absence of light pollution allows for a clear view of the constellations and the Milky Way.

Remember to come prepared for the desert environment with appropriate clothing, sunscreen, and plenty of water. It is also advisable to check weather conditions and plan your activities accordingly.

Visiting Regulations and Permits:
To enter Wadi Rum, visitors must purchase an entry ticket or a Jordan Pass, which includes entry to multiple Jordanian attractions, including Wadi Rum. The ticket grants access to the protected area and helps maintain and preserve the natural and cultural heritage of Wadi Rum.

Consider guided tours or hiring a local Bedouin guide to make the most of your visit to Wadi Rum. They possess in-depth knowledge of the area, its history, and its hidden gems, ensuring an enriching and memorable experience.

Chapter 7: Aqaba

Aqaba is a coastal city located in the southernmost part of Jordan, along the Red Sea. It is Jordan's only coastal city and serves as the country's gateway to the sea. Aqaba is known for its stunning beaches, crystal-clear waters, and vibrant marine life, making it a popular destination for beach lovers, water sports enthusiasts, and diving enthusiasts.

Beaches and Water Activities:
Aqaba boasts beautiful beaches with soft golden sands and clear turquoise waters. Visitors can relax on the beaches, soak up the sun, and enjoy swimming in the warm waters of the Red Sea. Numerous water activities are available, including snorkeling, scuba diving, jet skiing, paddleboarding, and boat tours. The coral reefs and diverse marine life make Aqaba a paradise for underwater exploration.

Coral Reefs and Marine Life:
The Red Sea is renowned for its vibrant coral reefs and diverse marine ecosystem. Aqaba offers excellent opportunities for snorkeling and scuba diving, allowing visitors to discover the stunning

underwater world. The coral reefs are home to an array of colorful fish, sea turtles, and other marine creatures. Whether you are a novice snorkeler or an experienced diver, Aqaba offers unforgettable experiences for all skill levels.

Historical and Cultural Attractions:
In addition to its natural beauty, Aqaba also has historical and cultural attractions that are worth exploring. The Aqaba Fort, also known as Aqaba Castle or Mamluk Castle, is a 14th-century fortress that offers panoramic views of the city and the Red Sea. The Aqaba Archaeological Museum displays artifacts from ancient civilizations that have inhabited the area, providing insights into the region's history.

Dining and Shopping:
Aqaba offers a variety of dining options where you can savor delicious Jordanian cuisine, fresh seafood, and international flavors. The city has a vibrant food scene, with restaurants, cafes, and street food stalls offering a wide range of culinary delights. Aqaba also has a bustling market, known as the Souk, where you can explore local handicrafts, spices, jewelry, and souvenirs.

Nearby Attractions:

Aqaba serves as a convenient base to explore other notable attractions in the region. Just a short drive away is Wadi Rum, a stunning desert landscape known for its unique rock formations and adventurous experiences. Petra, one of the New Seven Wonders of the World, is also within reach from Aqaba and can be visited on a day trip.

Entry Fees and Permits:

Aqaba is generally accessible to visitors without specific entry fees or permits. However, certain activities such as diving, boat tours, or visiting historical sites may have associated fees or entrance charges. It is advisable to check with specific providers, tour operators, or local authorities for the most up-to-date information on fees and permits.

Aqaba offers a perfect combination of stunning beaches, underwater exploration, cultural attractions, and easy access to nearby wonders. It is a must-visit destination for travelers seeking sun, sand, and unforgettable experiences along Jordan's Red Sea coast.

Chapter 8: The Dead Sea, Madaba and Mount Nebo

The Dead Sea:

The Dead Sea, located between Jordan to the east and Israel to the west, is a saltwater lake known for its high salt and mineral content. It is the lowest point on Earth, situated more than 400 meters below sea level. The Dead Sea's unique geographical features and mineral-rich waters make it a popular destination for tourists and those seeking therapeutic benefits.

Therapeutic Benefits:

The Dead Sea is renowned for its therapeutic properties, which are attributed to the high mineral content of its water and mud. The water contains a high concentration of salts, including magnesium, potassium, and calcium, along with minerals like bromide and sodium. The mud found along the shores is rich in minerals and is believed to have healing properties for various skin conditions and ailments. Visitors often indulge in a "mud bath" experience, covering themselves in the therapeutic mud and then rinsing off in the salty water.

Floating Experience:
Due to the high salt content, the water of the Dead Sea has a remarkable buoyancy. The density of the water makes it nearly impossible to sink, allowing visitors to effortlessly float on the surface. It's a unique and enjoyable experience to lie back and effortlessly float in the calm, mineral-rich waters. Many people consider it a bucket-list experience.

Scenic Beauty:
Apart from its therapeutic properties, the Dead Sea is also known for its scenic beauty. Surrounded by rugged mountains and desert landscapes, the contrast of the deep blue water against the stark desert creates a picturesque setting. The dramatic landscapes provide excellent opportunities for photography and enjoying the natural beauty of the region.

Resorts and Spas:
The shores of the Dead Sea are dotted with resorts and spas that cater to visitors seeking relaxation and wellness. These facilities often offer luxurious

amenities, such as private beach access, pools with mineral water, spa treatments, and therapeutic massages. Staying at one of these resorts provides a comfortable and rejuvenating experience.

Visiting Tips:

- Due to the extremely high salt content, it's important to avoid getting the water in your eyes or mouth, as it can cause discomfort.
- It is advisable not to shave for a few days before visiting the Dead Sea, as the water can cause stinging and irritation on freshly shaved skin.
- Stay hydrated and avoid swallowing the water, as the high salt content can be dehydrating.
- It is recommended to bring a hat, sunglasses, and sunscreen to protect yourself from the intense sun and heat.

Entry Fees and Permits:

Access to the Dead Sea is available through various resorts, public beaches, and nature reserves. Some resorts and facilities charge an entrance fee, while others may require bookings or reservations. It is advisable to check with specific locations or consult with local authorities for the most up-to-date information on entry fees and permits.

The Dead Sea offers a unique combination of natural beauty, relaxation, and therapeutic benefits, making it a must-visit destination for those seeking a truly rejuvenating and memorable experience in Jordan.

Madaba

Madaba is a small city in central Jordan known for its rich history and archaeological treasures. It has been inhabited since ancient times and holds significant importance for both religious and cultural reasons. Madaba is particularly famous for its Byzantine and Umayyad-era mosaics, which are among the finest in the region.

Mosaic Heritage:
Madaba is often referred to as the "City of Mosaics" due to its extraordinary collection of ancient mosaic artwork. The most famous mosaic in Madaba is the Madaba Map, also known as the Madaba Mosaic Map. This 6th-century mosaic map, located in the Greek Orthodox Church of St. George, depicts the Holy Land with Jerusalem at its center. It is the oldest known geographic map of the Holy Land and

provides valuable insights into the region's biblical and historical sites.

Churches and Religious Sites:
Madaba is home to several churches and religious sites of significance. In addition to the Church of St. George, which houses the Madaba Map, other notable churches include the Church of the Apostles and the Church of the Virgin Mary. These churches feature stunning mosaics that depict biblical scenes and religious motifs, showcasing the artistry and craftsmanship of the Byzantine period.

Archaeological Parks and Museums:
The Madaba Archaeological Park and the Madaba Museum are two essential sites for exploring the city's ancient history. The Archaeological Park houses the remains of Byzantine churches and houses, as well as a collection of mosaics discovered in the area. The museum displays a wide range of artifacts, including pottery, coins, and ancient sculptures, providing further insights into the city's past.

Crafts and Handicrafts:

Madaba is known for its traditional crafts and handicrafts. Visitors can explore workshops and galleries where artisans create and sell handmade pottery, glassware, mosaics, and jewelry. It's an excellent opportunity to witness the artistic traditions of the region and perhaps even purchase a unique piece as a souvenir.

Entry Fees and Permits:
The entry fees for specific sites in Madaba, such as the Church of St. George and the Madaba Archaeological Park, may vary. The fees are usually modest and allow access to multiple locations within the site. It is advisable to check with specific sites, local authorities, or tour operators for the most up-to-date information on entry fees and permits.

Madaba's ancient mosaics, religious sites, and cultural heritage make it a fascinating destination for history and art enthusiasts. Exploring Madaba offers a glimpse into the region's rich past and artistic traditions, making it a must-visit city on any itinerary in Jordan.

Mount Nebo

Mount Nebo is a significant site in Jordan, believed to be the place where Moses stood and viewed the Promised Land before his death according to biblical accounts. It holds immense religious importance for Christians, Jews, and Muslims alike. The mountain is mentioned in the Book of Deuteronomy in the Bible and is considered a sacred site for pilgrimage and reflection.

Biblical Connections:

Mount Nebo is mentioned in the Book of Deuteronomy, where Moses is said to have been granted a view of the Promised Land before he passed away. According to the Bible, this elevated vantage point allowed Moses to see the land that God had promised to the Israelites. For Christians, Mount Nebo is associated with Moses' final days and is considered a symbol of hope and faith.

Memorial of Moses:

At the summit of Mount Nebo, there is a memorial dedicated to Moses. The site features a sculpture of Moses and an ancient monastery, which has been restored and showcases Byzantine and early

Christian mosaics. The memorial serves as a pilgrimage destination for believers, offering a place for prayer, reflection, and contemplation.

Panoramic Views:
The summit of Mount Nebo offers breathtaking panoramic views of the Jordan Valley, the Dead Sea, and the surrounding landscapes. On clear days, it is even possible to see the distant skyline of Jerusalem. The stunning vistas from Mount Nebo provide visitors with an appreciation of the biblical landscapes and the natural beauty of the region.

Mosaic Artwork:
The ancient monastery on Mount Nebo houses remarkable mosaic artwork dating back to the 6th century AD. These Byzantine and early Christian mosaics depict biblical scenes, animals, and geometric patterns. The mosaics are well-preserved and provide a glimpse into the artistic and cultural heritage of the region during that time.

Exploring Mount Nebo:
Visitors to Mount Nebo can explore the memorial site, visit the ancient monastery, and admire the mosaics. There are viewing platforms that offer

unobstructed vistas, allowing visitors to take in the panoramic beauty of the surroundings. Additionally, there is a small museum on-site that provides further insights into the historical and religious significance of Mount Nebo.

Entry Fees and Permits:
 There is an entry fee to access the Mount Nebo site. The fee helps with the maintenance and preservation of the area. You can check with local authorities or tour operators for the most up-to-date information on entry fees and permits.

Mount Nebo's association with Moses, its panoramic vistas, and its ancient mosaics make it a compelling destination for religious and cultural exploration. It offers a unique opportunity to connect with the biblical narrative, appreciate the natural beauty of the region, and reflect on the enduring significance of faith and history.

Chapter 9: Dana Biosphere Reserve and Shobak Castle

Dana Biosphere Reserve

The Dana Biosphere Reserve is a unique natural and cultural heritage site located in southern Jordan. It is one of the largest nature reserves in the country, covering an area of over 300 square kilometers. The reserve encompasses diverse ecosystems, including mountains, canyons, valleys, and desert landscapes. It is home to a wide range of flora and fauna, as well as ancient archaeological sites and traditional Bedouin communities.

Biodiversity and Nature:
The Dana Biosphere Reserve boasts an impressive array of biodiversity, making it a haven for nature enthusiasts. The reserve is home to several rare and endangered species, including the Nubian ibex, Arabian oryx, and Syrian wolf. It also supports a variety of plant life, with over 700 species identified within its boundaries. Visitors to the reserve can explore hiking trails, birdwatching spots, and scenic

viewpoints to appreciate the natural beauty and ecological importance of the area.

Hiking and Outdoor Activities:
Dana Biosphere Reserve offers numerous hiking trails that cater to different levels of difficulty and interests. The trails take visitors through stunning landscapes, including the steep canyons of Wadi Dana and the rugged mountains of the Great Rift Valley. Hiking enthusiasts can enjoy panoramic vistas, encounter unique wildlife, and experience the tranquility of the wilderness. Other outdoor activities in the reserve include mountain biking, rock climbing, and camping under the starry desert sky.

Cultural Heritage and Bedouin Communities:
The Dana Biosphere Reserve is not only a natural treasure but also a cultural one. The reserve is home to several archaeological sites, including the ruins of Dana Village, a once-thriving settlement dating back to the Byzantine period. Visitors can explore the ancient stone houses, churches, and cisterns, gaining insights into the history and way of life of the past inhabitants. Additionally, the reserve is inhabited by traditional Bedouin communities whose way of life

is deeply connected to the natural environment. Interacting with the Bedouin people provides a unique cultural experience and an opportunity to learn about their traditions and customs.

Conservation and Sustainable Tourism:
The Dana Biosphere Reserve is managed by the Royal Society for the Conservation of Nature (RSCN) and has a strong focus on conservation and sustainable tourism practices. The RSCN works to protect the biodiversity and cultural heritage of the reserve while promoting responsible tourism that benefits local communities. By visiting the reserve, travelers support conservation efforts and contribute to the sustainable development of the region.

Entry Fees: Entry fees for the Dana Biosphere Reserve vary depending on the type of visit and activities. It is recommended to contact the reserve's management for the most up-to-date information.

Permits: A permit is required to enter the Dana Biosphere Reserve. You can obtain it at the visitor center or arrange it through a local tour operator.

The Dana Biosphere Reserve offers a unique opportunity to immerse oneself in the beauty of nature, experience local culture, and support conservation efforts. It is an ideal destination for nature lovers, adventure enthusiasts, and those seeking an authentic and sustainable travel experience in Jordan.

Shobak Castle

Shobak Castle, also known as Montreal or Mont Real, is a historic fortress located in the town of Shobak in southern Jordan. It was constructed in the 12th century by the Crusaders under the orders of King Baldwin I of Jerusalem. The castle was built to control the trade routes and provide a stronghold against potential Muslim armies.

Architecture and Design:
Shobak Castle is a fine example of Crusader military architecture. It is situated on a hilltop, offering a commanding view of the surrounding landscapes. The castle features thick defensive walls, towers, and a central courtyard. The construction materials used include local limestone, giving the castle its distinctive appearance. The design incorporates both

defensive and residential elements, highlighting the balance between military functionality and living quarters.

Defensive Features:
The castle was strategically designed with various defensive features. Its elevated position on the hill provided a vantage point for surveillance and defense. The fortress is surrounded by sturdy walls with arrow slits and battlements for archers to repel attackers. The castle also features towers for lookout purposes and a fortified gatehouse to control access to the castle.

Historical Significance:
Shobak Castle served as a strategic Crusader stronghold in the region. It played a significant role in the defense of the Kingdom of Jerusalem and the protection of the trade routes between Egypt and Syria. The castle changed hands multiple times throughout history, witnessing conflicts between Crusaders, Ayyubids, and Mamluks. Its historical significance lies in its association with the Crusader period and its role in the events of the time.

Exploring the Castle:

Visitors to Shobak Castle can explore its various sections and experience the atmosphere of a medieval fortress. The castle offers panoramic views of the surrounding countryside, allowing visitors to appreciate the strategic positioning of the fortress. Within the castle, visitors can walk along the walls, explore the interior spaces, and climb the towers for a closer look at the architecture and views.

Entry Fees: the entry fee for Shobak Castle is about 2 JOD per person.

Permits: No specific permits are required for visiting Shobak Castle.

Shobak Castle offers a captivating journey into the Crusader period and provides an opportunity to explore the rich history of the region. Its impressive architecture, panoramic views, and historical importance make it an intriguing destination for history enthusiasts and those interested in the Crusader legacy in the Middle East.

Chapter 10: Umm Qais, Ajloun Castle and Ma'in Hot Springs

Umm Qais

Umm Qais, also known as Gadara in ancient times, is an archaeological site located in the northwestern part of Jordan, near the borders of Israel and Syria. It was once a thriving Greco-Roman city and played a significant role in the ancient Decapolis league. Umm Qais offers visitors a chance to explore the remains of this ancient city and learn about its historical and cultural significance.

Roman Ruins:

Umm Qais is renowned for its well-preserved Roman ruins, which provide insights into the city's past. Visitors can explore the ancient theater, which offers stunning views of the surrounding landscapes and neighboring countries. The theater is known for its impressive acoustics and is still used today for performances and events. Other notable ruins include the colonnaded street, temples, a basilica, and a nymphaeum (a public fountain).

Panoramic Views:

One of the main attractions of Umm Qais is its breathtaking panoramic views. The site is situated on a hilltop overlooking the Sea of Galilee (Lake Tiberias), the Golan Heights, and the Jordan Valley. The stunning vistas offer a glimpse into the diverse landscapes of the region and provide a picturesque backdrop for exploring the ancient ruins.

Cultural and Historical Significance:

Umm Qais holds great cultural and historical significance due to its role as a prominent city in the Greco-Roman era. It was a center of Hellenistic culture and trade and became part of the Decapolis league, a group of ten cities that were heavily influenced by Greek and Roman civilizations. The ruins at Umm Qais provide a tangible connection to this ancient past, offering visitors a chance to step back in time and imagine the city's former grandeur.

Archaeological Museum:

Umm Qais is also home to an archaeological museum that displays a collection of artifacts uncovered during excavations. The museum showcases a variety of objects, including statues, mosaics, pottery, and coins, which provide further insights into the daily life and culture of the people who lived in Gadara.

Local Culture and Hospitality:
Visitors to Umm Qais have the opportunity to interact with the local community and experience Jordanian hospitality. The town of Umm Qais itself offers a glimpse into the daily life of the local residents, with its narrow streets, traditional houses, and local markets. It is a chance to connect with the local culture and sample traditional Jordanian cuisine.

Entry Fees and Permits:
The entry fee to access the archaeological site and museum at Umm Qais is about 5 JOD per person. The fee contributes to the maintenance and preservation of the site. However, check with local authorities or tour operators for the most up-to-date information on entry fees and permits.

Umm Qais offers a unique opportunity to delve into the ancient world, appreciate the architectural marvels of the Roman era, and soak in the stunning vistas of the surrounding landscapes. It is a must-visit destination for history enthusiasts, culture seekers, and anyone interested in exploring the diverse historical heritage of Jordan.

Ajloun Castle

Ajloun Castle, also known as Qal'at Ar-Rabad, is a 12th-century fortress located in the town of Ajloun in northern Jordan. It was built by the Ayyubid ruler Salah ad-Din al-Ayyubi (Saladin) to protect the region against Crusader attacks and to control the iron mines in the area. The castle played a crucial role in defending the surrounding territory and served as a strategic stronghold during medieval times.

Architecture and Design:
Ajloun Castle is an impressive example of Islamic military architecture. The fortress is perched atop a hill, providing a commanding view of the surrounding countryside. Its design incorporates both defensive and residential elements, with thick walls, towers, and a central courtyard. The castle's strategic location allowed its occupants to monitor and control the nearby routes and access points.

Defensive Features:
The castle was designed with several defensive features to protect against potential threats. Its strategic position on the hill provided a vantage point for surveillance and defense. The castle's thick stone walls and towers offered protection against enemy attacks, while arrow slits and battlements allowed defenders to repel invaders. Inside the castle, there are also underground chambers that served as storage areas and shelters.

Historical Significance:
Ajloun Castle played a significant role in the defense of the region during the Crusader era. It was part of a network of fortresses that protected the lands from Crusader incursions. The castle's strategic location helped in safeguarding the surrounding areas and controlling the nearby trade routes. It stands as a testament to the military and architectural prowess of the Ayyubid dynasty during the medieval period.

Exploring the Castle:
Visitors to Ajloun Castle can explore its various sections, including the towers, courtyards, and underground chambers. The castle offers panoramic

views of the Ajloun countryside, providing a glimpse into the historical landscape. Within the castle, there is also a small museum that displays artifacts and exhibits related to the castle's history and the region's past.

Surrounding Nature Reserve, including oak trees, wildflowers, and various bird species. Visitors to the castle can combine their visit with a nature excursion, allowing them to experience both history and nature in one trip.

Entry Fees and Permits:
The entry fee to access Ajloun Castle is about 2 JOD per person. But, be sure to check with local authorities or tour operators for the most up-to-date information on entry fees and permits.

Ajloun Castle stands as a remarkable testament to Jordan's medieval history and serves as a reminder of the region's strategic importance during ancient times. Its architectural beauty, historical significance, and the opportunity to combine the visit with nature exploration make it an intriguing destination for history enthusiasts and nature lovers alike.

Ma'in Hot Springs

Ma'in Hot Springs, also known as Hammamat Ma'in, is a series of natural hot springs located in the Ma'in Valley in Jordan. It is situated approximately 58 kilometers southwest of Amman, the capital city. The hot springs are nestled amidst stunning natural surroundings, surrounded by steep cliffs and lush greenery. The area offers a tranquil and picturesque setting for relaxation and rejuvenation.

Hot Springs and Waterfalls:
Ma'in Hot Springs are renowned for their therapeutic and mineral-rich waters. The springs originate from underground volcanic hot water streams and emerge at various temperatures, ranging from warm to hot. Visitors can enjoy the natural hot pools, which are said to have healing properties and are known for their soothing effects on the body and mind. The springs cascade down a series of waterfalls, creating a beautiful and calming ambiance.

Resort Facilities and Spas:
There are several resorts and spas in the Ma'in Hot Springs area that cater to visitors seeking a luxurious

and rejuvenating experience. These establishments offer a range of facilities, including hot spring pools, spa treatments, massage therapies, and wellness programs. Visitors can indulge in thermal baths, mud wraps, and various therapies that harness the healing properties of the hot springs.

Panoramic Views and Hiking:
In addition to the hot springs, Ma'in Valley offers breathtaking panoramic views of the surrounding landscapes. Visitors can take in the beauty of the valley, with its rugged mountains, terraced hillsides, and waterfalls. The area is also suitable for hiking, allowing visitors to explore the natural beauty of the valley and discover hidden gems along the trails.

Cultural and Historical Significance:
Ma'in Hot Springs have a rich historical and cultural significance. They have been known and used for their healing properties since ancient times. The hot springs are mentioned in biblical texts and were frequented by historical figures such as Herod the Great and King Herod Antipas. The area is also home to the ruins of Ma'in Palace, an ancient bathhouse believed to have been used by the Roman rulers.

Entry Fees: Entry fees for Ma'in Hot Springs vary depending on the facilities and services you choose. It is advisable to check with the resort or spa you plan to visit for accurate pricing.

Permits: No specific permits are required for visiting Ma'in Hot Springs

Ma'in Hot Springs offer a unique opportunity to relax, unwind, and immerse oneself in the natural healing properties of the thermal waters. The combination of therapeutic benefits, stunning natural landscapes, and luxurious spa facilities make it an ideal destination for wellness seekers and those looking to experience the beauty of Jordan's natural wonders.

Chapter 11: Dining and Local Cuisine

The culinary scene in Jordan is vibrant and diverse, offering a wide range of flavors and culinary experiences. Jordanian cuisine reflects the country's rich history, cultural diversity, and geographical location. Here are some key aspects of Jordan's culinary and gastronomic scene:

Traditional Jordanian Cuisine: Jordanian cuisine is deeply rooted in Bedouin traditions and local ingredients. It features a variety of dishes prepared with simple yet flavorful ingredients such as olive oil, herbs, spices, grains, and vegetables. Traditional dishes like Mansaf, Falafel, Maqluba, and Shawarma showcase the authentic flavors of Jordan.

Regional Variations: Jordan's regional diversity is also reflected in its cuisine. Different regions in Jordan have their own culinary specialties and variations. For example, in the north, you'll find dishes like Mansaf and Sujuk (spicy sausages), while the south is known for its spicier flavors and dishes like Shish Barak (meat-filled dumplings in yogurt sauce).

Street Food Culture: Jordan has a vibrant street food culture, particularly in cities like Amman. Exploring the bustling street food markets and stalls allows visitors to savor a variety of delicious and affordable dishes. Some popular street foods include falafel, shawarma, knafeh (a sweet pastry), and freshly squeezed juices.

Arabic and International Influences: Jordanian cuisine has been influenced by neighboring countries and the wider Middle Eastern region. You'll find elements of Levantine, Palestinian, Syrian, and Iraqi cuisines in Jordanian dishes. Additionally, international influences have made their way into the culinary scene, with a growing number of restaurants offering international cuisines such as Italian, Asian, and Mediterranean.

Farm-to-Table and Locally Sourced Ingredients: Jordan's agricultural landscape is rich and diverse, producing a variety of fruits, vegetables, herbs, and grains. The farm-to-table concept has gained popularity, with many restaurants sourcing their ingredients locally and focusing on seasonality and sustainability.

Fine Dining and Fusion Cuisine: Alongside traditional and street food, Jordan also offers a growing fine dining scene. Upscale restaurants in major cities like Amman blend traditional Jordanian flavors with modern techniques, offering a fusion of international and local cuisines.

Traditional Jordanian Dishes:

Certainly! As a tour guide, I would be delighted to introduce you to some traditional Jordanian dishes:

1. Mansaf: Considered the national dish of Jordan, Mansaf is a hearty and festive meal. It consists of tender lamb cooked in a fermented yogurt sauce called jameed, which gives it a tangy flavor. The lamb is typically served on a large platter over a bed of rice and garnished with toasted nuts and fresh herbs. Mansaf is often enjoyed during special occasions and family gatherings.

2. Falafel: Falafel is a popular Middle Eastern dish made from ground chickpeas or fava beans mixed with herbs and spices. The mixture is shaped into small patties or balls and deep-fried until crispy and golden brown. Falafel is commonly served in pita bread with tahini sauce, along with fresh vegetables and pickles. It is a beloved street food in Jordan and can also be found in many restaurants.

3. Maqluba: Maqluba, meaning "upside-down" in Arabic, is a delicious one-pot dish that is both visually stunning and flavorful. It is prepared by layering rice, meat (such as chicken, lamb, or beef), and an assortment of vegetables, such as cauliflower, eggplant, and potatoes, in a pot. The dish is then cooked until the ingredients are tender, and the pot is inverted onto a serving platter, creating a beautiful presentation.

4. Zarb: Zarb is a traditional Bedouin style of cooking that involves roasting meat and vegetables underground. A shallow pit is dug, and a fire is built at the bottom. Marinated meat, usually lamb or chicken, is placed on top of a rack, while vegetables like potatoes, carrots, and onions are added as well. The pit is then covered with hot embers and sand, allowing the food to slowly cook and infuse with smoky flavors.

5. Makloubeh: Makloubeh, which means "upside-down" in Arabic, is a flavorful and comforting dish. It typically consists of layers of meat (such as chicken or lamb), rice, and a variety of vegetables, including eggplant, cauliflower, and carrots. The dish is cooked in a pot, and when ready to serve, it is flipped upside down onto a large platter, with the meat and vegetables on top and the rice at the bottom.

6. Sfiha: Sfiha is a popular Jordanian appetizer or snack. It is a type of open-faced meat pie topped with a mixture of ground meat (usually lamb or beef) and spices, such as onions, tomatoes, and various herbs. The meat topping is typically seasoned with flavors like cinnamon, allspice, and sumac. Sfiha is often enjoyed with a squeeze of lemon juice and can be found in bakeries and street food stalls.

7. Shawarma: Shawarma is a popular street food in Jordan and throughout the Middle East. It consists of thinly sliced marinated meat, usually chicken or lamb, which is slow-roasted on a vertical spit. The meat is then shaved off and served in a warm pita bread with a variety of toppings and sauces, such as tahini, garlic sauce, pickles, and vegetables.

8. Jordanian Mezze: Mezze is a collection of small dishes that are served as appetizers or as a complete meal. Jordanian mezze includes a wide variety of dishes, such as hummus (a dip made from mashed chickpeas, tahini, garlic, and lemon juice), baba ganoush (a smoky eggplant dip), tabbouleh (a refreshing salad made with bulgur wheat, parsley, tomatoes, and mint), fattoush (a mixed vegetable salad with toasted bread), and moutabel (a spiced eggplant dip).

9. Kofta: Kofta refers to seasoned ground meat, typically beef or lamb, that is shaped into long, cylindrical patties or kebabs and grilled or baked. The meat is seasoned with a mixture of herbs, spices, and onions, giving it a flavorful taste. Kofta is often served with rice, bread, or as part of a mezze platter.

10. Warak Enab: Warak Enab, also known as stuffed grape leaves or dolma, is a dish made of rolled grape leaves filled with a mixture of rice, minced meat, herbs, and spices. The rolls are then simmered in a flavorful broth until tender. Warak Enab can be served as a main dish or as part of a mezze spread.

11. Jordanian Desserts: Jordanian cuisine offers a variety of delicious desserts. One popular sweet treat is Knafeh, made with shredded phyllo dough, cheese, and sweet syrup. Another popular dessert is Atayef, which are small pancakes filled with a sweet cream or nut mixture and then folded and fried. Other notable desserts include Baklava, Halawet El Jibn (a sweet cheese pastry), and Awama (small deep-fried dough balls coated in syrup).

These are just a few of the traditional dishes you'll find in Jordan. These dishes represent a diverse range of flavors and textures that showcase the culinary traditions of Jordan. Exploring the local cuisine and trying these traditional dishes is an essential part of experiencing Jordanian culture.

Popular Restaurants and Street Food Markets:

Jordan has a vibrant culinary scene with numerous popular restaurants and street food markets where you can savor the flavors of the country. Here are some noteworthy options to consider:

Popular Restaurants in Jordan:

1. Hashem Restaurant (Amman): Located in downtown Amman, Hashem Restaurant is an iconic eatery that has been serving delicious and affordable Middle Eastern food since 1952. It is particularly famous for its falafel, hummus, and freshly baked bread.

2. Tawaheen al-Hawa (Amman): Tawaheen al-Hawa, meaning "The Windmill," is a renowned Jordanian restaurant that specializes in authentic Bedouin cuisine. The restaurant offers a unique dining experience in a traditional tent setting, where you can enjoy dishes like Mansaf, Zarb, and grilled meats.

3. Sufra Restaurant (Amman): Sufra Restaurant showcases traditional Jordanian cuisine in a contemporary setting. It offers a variety of dishes, including Mansaf, Makloubeh, and a wide range of mezze. The restaurant also provides a cozy atmosphere and beautiful views of Amman.

4. Fakhr El-Din (Amman): Fakhr El-Din is a high-end restaurant that serves Lebanese and Middle Eastern cuisine. Located in the luxurious Le Royal Hotel, the restaurant offers an extensive menu of traditional dishes, grilled meats, and seafood, along with a refined dining experience.

5. Tannoureen (Jerash): Situated in the ancient city of Jerash, Tannoureen is a popular restaurant known for its traditional Jordanian and Levantine dishes. It offers a charming outdoor setting where you can enjoy flavorful dishes while taking in the historic surroundings.

6. Beit Sitti (Amman): Beit Sitti, which means "My Grandma's House" in Arabic, offers a unique culinary experience where you can learn to cook traditional Jordanian dishes in a cozy and welcoming atmosphere. The restaurant provides

106

cooking classes followed by a delicious meal prepared by the participants.

7. Haret Jdoudna (Madaba): Located in the historic town of Madaba, Haret Jdoudna is a charming restaurant housed in a traditional Jordanian house. It serves a variety of traditional Jordanian and Middle Eastern dishes, with an emphasis on local ingredients and flavors.

8. Kan Zaman (Amman): Kan Zaman, situated in a restored historic building, offers a cultural and dining experience with its traditional Jordanian cuisine and live music performances. The restaurant has a beautiful outdoor terrace overlooking Amman's skyline.

9. Wild Jordan Center (Amman): The Wild Jordan Center is a sustainable tourism initiative that features a restaurant offering panoramic views of Amman. It serves a selection of locally sourced and organic dishes, showcasing Jordanian flavors with a modern twist.

Street Food Markets in Jordan:

1. Rainbow Street (Amman): Rainbow Street is a vibrant street in Amman known for its food stalls, cafes, and souvenir shops. You'll find a variety of street food options here, including falafel, shawarma, knafeh, and freshly squeezed juices.

2. Al-Balad Market (Amman): Al-Balad Market, also known as the Downtown Market, is a bustling area where you can explore traditional markets and sample street food. It offers a wide range of culinary delights, from grilled meats and local sweets to freshly brewed tea.

3. Al-Hussein Square (Amman): Al-Hussein Square, located near the King Hussein Mosque, is a popular spot for street food. You can indulge in Jordanian specialties like falafel, shawarma, and traditional sweets while experiencing the vibrant atmosphere of the area.

4. Al-Khobz Al-Hafi Bakery (Madaba): Al-Khobz Al-Hafi Bakery is a famous bakery in Madaba known for its freshly baked bread. You can grab a loaf of warm bread and pair it with local cheeses, olives, and dips for a delicious and authentic snack.

5. Souk Jara (Amman): Souk Jara is a seasonal market held during the summer months in Amman. It features local vendors selling crafts, clothing, and, of course, a variety of street food. It's a great place to sample traditional Jordanian dishes while enjoying live music and entertainment.

6. Souk Al-Sukar (Amman): Souk Al-Sukar, meaning "Sugar Market," is a bustling market in downtown Amman known for its vibrant atmosphere and diverse food stalls. It's a great place to sample Jordanian street food like grilled meats, shawarma, falafel, and Arabic sweets.

7. Souk Al-Salt (Salt): Located in the historic town of Salt, Souk Al-Salt is a traditional market where you can experience the local flavors and street food culture. It offers a variety of snacks and treats, including traditional Jordanian bread, pastries, and local specialties.

8. Ajloun Street Food Market (Ajloun): Ajloun, a city in northern Jordan, has a vibrant street food scene. The street food market offers a range of local snacks and delicacies, allowing you to immerse yourself in the flavors of northern Jordan.

Whether you're seeking traditional Jordanian cuisine or street food experiences, these restaurants and markets offer a taste of authentic Jordanian flavors and hospitality.

Chapter 12: Shopping and Souvenirs

Jordan is known for its vibrant markets and souks where you can find unique Jordanian products, traditional clothing, spices, ceramics, and jewelry. Here are some of the best markets and handicraft stores to visit:

1. Al-Balad Market (Downtown Amman): Located in downtown Amman, Al-Balad Market is a bustling hub of shops and stalls where you can find a variety of traditional Jordanian products. Here, you can explore shops selling textiles, spices, jewelry, traditional clothing, ceramics, and souvenirs. The market is particularly known for its vibrant atmosphere and local crafts.

2. Souk Jara (Amman): Souk Jara is a seasonal market that takes place during the summer months in Amman. It showcases a wide range of handmade crafts, including textiles, ceramics, jewelry, leather goods, and traditional clothing. This market is a great place to find unique and authentic Jordanian products directly from local artisans.

3. Rainbow Street (Amman): Rainbow Street is not only famous for its food stalls but also for its charming boutiques and shops. Here, you can find a selection of local products, including traditional clothing, spices, ceramics, and jewelry. The street offers a mix of modern and traditional shops, allowing you to explore contemporary designs and traditional craftsmanship.

4. Souk by the Sea (Aqaba): Souk by the Sea is a popular market located in Aqaba, a coastal city in Jordan. It offers a variety of shops selling local handicrafts, including jewelry, textiles, spices, and traditional clothing. This market provides a unique shopping experience with a view of the Red Sea and a laid-back atmosphere.

5. The Duke's Diwan (Amman): The Duke's Diwan is a renowned handicraft store in Amman that showcases a wide range of Jordanian and Middle Eastern crafts. Here, you can find handwoven textiles, intricate embroidery, traditional clothing, ceramics, and jewelry. The store is known for promoting local artisans and supporting traditional craftsmanship.

6. Darat al Funun (Amman): Darat al Funun is an arts and cultural center in Amman that features a gallery and a gift shop. The gift shop offers a selection of unique and high-quality handmade crafts, including ceramics, textiles, paintings, and jewelry. It's an excellent place to find artistic and contemporary Jordanian creations.

7. Downtown Salt (Salt): The historic town of Salt, located northwest of Amman, is known for its charming streets and traditional architecture. The downtown area of Salt is home to various shops and boutiques where you can find traditional clothing, handmade crafts, ceramics, and local products.

8. Abu Shakra Market (Amman): Abu Shakra Market is a traditional market in Amman that specializes in textiles and fabrics. Here, you can find a wide range of fabrics, including colorful Bedouin textiles, embroidered garments, and traditional Jordanian clothing. It's a great place to shop for unique fabrics to create your own clothing or home decor items.

9. The Souk (Madaba): Located in the heart of Madaba, The Souk is a bustling market known for its selection of handicrafts and souvenirs. You can find a variety of traditional Jordanian products, including mosaic art, ceramics, pottery, woven baskets, and traditional embroidered items. The market offers a glimpse into Madaba's rich cultural heritage and craftsmanship.

10. Um Qais Crafts Cooperative (Umm Qais): In the town of Umm Qais, you can visit the Um Qais Crafts Cooperative, a community-based initiative that promotes local artisans and their crafts. The cooperative showcases a range of handmade products, including ceramics, olive wood crafts, textiles, and jewelry. It's a wonderful place to support local artists and purchase authentic Jordanian handicrafts.

11. Jordan River Foundation Showroom (Amman): The Jordan River Foundation Showroom is a social enterprise that supports local artisans and their handmade products. Here, you can find a variety of high-quality crafts, including handmade jewelry, textiles, accessories, and home decor items.

Shopping at this showroom helps empower local communities and contribute to social development projects.

12. The Souk at Petra (Petra): Located near the entrance of the ancient city of Petra, The Souk offers a unique shopping experience amidst the breathtaking archaeological site. Here, you can find shops selling traditional Bedouin jewelry, handcrafted silverware, spices, and Bedouin textiles. It's an opportunity to immerse yourself in the history and culture of Petra while exploring unique Jordanian products.

13. The Craftsman House (Amman): The Craftsman House is a boutique store that showcases the work of local artisans and craftsmen from across Jordan. The store offers a curated collection of handmade products, including pottery, glassware, jewelry, textiles, and woodwork. It's a great place to discover authentic Jordanian crafts and support local artists.

14. Al-Karak Souk (Karak): The city of Karak is known for its historic castle, but it also has a bustling souk where you can find a range of local products. The souk offers shops selling traditional clothing, spices, ceramics, handmade soaps, and local delicacies. It's a great place to experience the local market culture and find unique souvenirs.

15. The Souk at Aqaba (Aqaba): Aqaba's main market area, known as "The Souk," offers a variety of shops and stalls selling local products and souvenirs. You can browse through stores offering spices, dried fruits, traditional clothing, handmade crafts, and jewelry. It's an ideal place to shop for authentic Jordanian products while enjoying the vibrant atmosphere of Aqaba.

When visiting these markets and stores, you can interact with local artisans, learn about the craftsmanship behind the products, and support the local economy. It's always a good idea to engage in friendly bargaining and take your time exploring to find the perfect unique Jordanian products to bring back as souvenirs or gifts.

Chapter 13: Local Events and Festivals

Jordan is a country rich in cultural heritage and traditions, which are showcased through various annual events, cultural festivals, and celebrations. Here are a few notable ones:

1. Jerash Festival: Held annually in July, the Jerash Festival is a renowned cultural event that takes place in the ancient city of Jerash. It features music concerts, dance performances, theatrical shows, and art exhibitions, attracting both local and international artists. This festival provides a unique opportunity to witness the vibrant cultural scene of Jordan.

2. Petra By Night: Experience the magic of Petra by attending the enchanting Petra By Night event. Held several times a week, visitors have the chance to walk through the ancient city of Petra by candlelight. As you follow the candle-lit path, you'll be surrounded by the stunning rock-cut architecture, creating a truly magical and unforgettable experience.

3. Amman Citadel Nights: During the summer months, Amman Citadel Nights takes place at the Amman Citadel, offering visitors a glimpse into Jordanian culture and heritage. This event features traditional music performances, dance shows, and art exhibitions, providing a platform for local artists to showcase their talent. It's a fantastic opportunity to immerse yourself in the local culture while enjoying the beautiful setting of the Amman Citadel.

4. Al-Balad Music Festival: Celebrating Jordanian and Arab music, the Al-Balad Music Festival takes place in Amman and various cities across the country. This festival brings together renowned musicians and singers who perform a variety of music genres, including traditional Arab music, contemporary Arabic pop, and fusion styles. It's a must-attend event for music lovers.

5. Eid Al-Fitr and Eid Al-Adha: The two most important religious holidays in Jordan are Eid Al-Fitr and Eid Al-Adha. Eid Al-Fitr marks the end of Ramadan, the holy month of fasting, and is

118

celebrated with family gatherings, feasts, and giving gifts. Eid Al-Adha commemorates the willingness of Ibrahim (Abraham) to sacrifice his son and is observed with prayers, animal sacrifices, and sharing of meat with the less fortunate.

6. Jordan Handicrafts Festival: Showcasing the rich heritage of Jordanian craftsmanship, the Jordan Handicrafts Festival is a major event that takes place in Amman. Local artisans from different regions of Jordan gather to exhibit and sell their traditional crafts, including pottery, textiles, woodwork, and jewelry. It's a wonderful opportunity to purchase unique souvenirs and support local artisans.

7. Aqaba Traditional Arts Festival: Held in the city of Aqaba, this festival showcases the traditional arts and crafts of the region. Visitors can witness demonstrations of traditional weaving, pottery making, and other crafts, as well as enjoy cultural performances and music. It's a great way to learn about the unique heritage of Aqaba and its surrounding areas.

8. Jordan Rally: For motorsport enthusiasts, the Jordan Rally is a thrilling event held as part of the

FIA World Rally Championship. The rally takes place in various locations across the country and attracts top rally drivers from around the world. It's an exhilarating experience to watch the high-speed cars maneuver through challenging terrains.

9. Madaba Mosaic Festival: Madaba, known as the "City of Mosaics," hosts an annual Mosaic Festival that celebrates the artistry and history of mosaic-making. The festival features exhibitions, workshops, and guided tours of the city's famous mosaic artworks. Visitors can witness the intricate mosaic craftsmanship and even try their hand at creating their own mosaic pieces.

10. Amman International Theatre Festival: Theater enthusiasts should not miss the Amman International Theatre Festival, which brings together local and international theater groups to showcase their talent. The festival features a diverse range of performances, including plays, musicals, and experimental theater, providing a platform for cultural exchange and creative expression.

11. Jordan Food Week: Food lovers can indulge in the culinary delights of Jordan during Jordan Food

Week. This annual event showcases the country's diverse gastronomy, from traditional Jordanian dishes to international cuisines. Visitors can explore food stalls, attend cooking demonstrations, and savor a wide variety of delicious dishes prepared by local chefs and food vendors.

12. Um Qais Summer Festival: Located in the northern part of Jordan, Um Qais hosts a summer festival that celebrates the cultural heritage of the region. The festival features traditional music and dance performances, art exhibitions, and local food stalls. Visitors can immerse themselves in the unique traditions and folklore of the area while enjoying the beautiful scenery.

These events and festivals highlight the vibrant cultural scene in Jordan and offer visitors a chance to engage with the country's rich heritage, traditions, and art forms. Attending these celebrations provides a deeper understanding of Jordanian culture and creates lasting memories of your visit.

Conclusion

As your journey through the enchanting landscapes of Jordan comes to an end, it is impossible not to be overwhelmed by a flood of emotions. The experiences you've had, the people you've met, and the places you've explored have woven themselves into the fabric of your being, leaving an indelible mark on your heart.

The ancient ruins of Petra, the vast expanse of Wadi Rum, the bustling streets of Amman, and the warm hospitality of the Jordanian people have touched your soul in ways you never imagined. The rich tapestry of history, culture, and natural beauty has unfolded before your eyes, revealing the hidden treasures of this remarkable country.

But it is not just the breathtaking sights and captivating stories that have moved you. It is the connection you've formed with the land and its people. The kindness and generosity that have been extended to you, the moments of shared laughter and shared meals, have bridged the gaps of language and culture, reminding you of our common humanity.

As you bid farewell to Jordan, a part of you remains behind, intertwined with the memories and experiences that have forever changed you. You carry with you the spirit of the desert winds, the echoes of ancient civilizations, and the warmth of the Jordanian people.

Jordan is not just a destination; it is an emotional journey. It is a place that touches your heart, stirs your soul, and leaves you with a sense of wonder and gratitude. It is a place where you have witnessed the resilience and beauty of a nation that has overcome challenges and preserved its heritage with unwavering pride.

As you venture back to your everyday life, you know that a piece of Jordan will forever dwell within you. You will cherish the moments, the connections, and the lessons learned. And you will carry the spirit of Jordan, inspiring you to embrace new adventures, embrace diversity, and embrace the beauty of the world.

In the end, Jordan is more than a travel destination; it is an emotional awakening. It is a place where the past and the present converge, where stories are whispered through the ancient ruins, and where the echoes of a vibrant culture resonate in every corner. It is a place that leaves an everlasting imprint on your heart, beckoning you to return and discover even more of its magic.

Glossary

Useful Phrases

As a tourist in Jordan, learning a few common Arabic phrases can greatly enhance your communication and interaction with locals. Here are some useful phrases:

1. Greetings:
   - Hello: Marhaba
   - Good morning: Sabah al-khair
   - Good evening: Masaa' al-khair
   - How are you?: Kayf halak?
   - I'm fine, thank you: Ana bekhair, shukran

2. Basic Expressions:
   - Yes: Na'am
   - No: La
   - Please: Min fadlak (to a male) / Min fadlik (to a female)
   - Thank you: Shukran
   - You're welcome: Afwan
   - Excuse me: Law samaht

- I'm sorry: Ana asif
- Goodbye: Ma'a as-salama

3. Asking for Help:
    - Can you help me?: Mumkin tesaa'dni?
    - Where is...?: Ain...?
    - I'm lost: Tawalat/ta'atalt
    - I need a taxi: Biddi taxi
    - How much does it cost?: Kam hatha?
    - Can you speak English?: Mumkin tehki ingli

Printed in Great Britain
by Amazon